Don't Let Christians Keep You From Jesus Christ

By: Steven Kasper

Scripture reference taken from The NIV Study Bible, New International Version, published by Zondervan Publishing House copyright 1984 by the International Bible Society.

Copyright © 2006 Steven J. Kasper

All rights reserved. No part of this publication may be reproduced, stored in a retrieval system, or transmitted in any form or by any means, electronic, mechanical, photocopying, recording, or otherwise, without the prior written permission of the publisher.

ISBN: 1-933899-13-1

Published by:
Holy Fire Publishing
531 Constitution Blvd., Martinsburg, WV 25401
www.ChristianPublish.com

Cover Design: Jay Cookingham

Printed in the United States of America and the United Kingdom

Dedicated to:

My friend, counselor, confidante
And Savior

Jesus Christ

"Who I think is getting a bad rap these days"

Table of Contents

Introduction

Chapter 1	*Faith or Fiction*
Chapter 2	*Who is the who in "Whoever"*
Chapter 3	*Lose the labels*
Chapter 4	*Junk the jargon*
Chapter 5	*Dump the denominations*
Chapter 6	*See your self*
Chapter 7	*Meet the Master*
Chapter 8	*Test the testimony*
Chapter 9	*Be a believer*
Chapter 10	*Forgive the forgiven*
Chapter 11	*Fan the flame*
Chapter 12	*Light the light*
Appendix	*Meeting Jesus, taking a walk down the road!*

Introduction

Mathew 9:13
"For I have not come to call the righteous, but sinners"

About 20 years ago I had a fairly new relationship with my friend Jesus. I was attending a church which was strongly based on the teachings of the Bible. Some of the people of the church were looking for a way to meet and get to know other people in the community so we could invite them to our small, but "we thought" friendly church.

At the time there was a slow pitch softball league in the city and another" Bible believing" church had a team. They were looking for some additional players. So the Pastor of our church, and a few of us weekend athletes, decided to help them fill out their roster.

It sounded like the ideal way to meet people and show them just how nice and friendly we were. The Pastor of the other church was the pitcher on the team and his son was the star shortstop. They were both pretty good players, however the problem was they were also both very bad sports.

They were constantly yelling and *"swearing"* at each other and the umpires as well. They scrapped for every advantage they could find and alienated not just the players on the other teams but the fans as well.

But wouldn't you know it; we actually had a pretty good team. Our record for the season was about 10 and 2 and we ended up playing the last game of the season for the championship. Here we were, two churches comprising a softball team in a city league, and just about every person in the stands, with the exception of our wives and relatives were rooting AGAINST us. Fortunately, we lost. But the cheers for our demise still ring in my ears.

Essentially, we were Christians giving my friend Jesus a bad name. That was twenty years ago, and I wish I could say that things are a lot better. But if anything, they are worse. Last month, my wife, Laura and I attended a huge Christian conference in a large Midwestern city. While we were at a mall attached to the conference center, my wife overheard two teenage girls refer to the center as *"that Christian lair"*. I like to think of myself as an optimist, but that did not sound like a compliment.

Author Phillip Yancy tells a story in his book *"What's So Amazing about Grace"*, of how he conducted an unscientific survey of people who sat next to him on airline flights. He told them that he was a journalist and that he was doing an article about Evangelical Christians, and he asked them what was the first thing that came to their mind when he mentioned that description to them. He said if you were an Evangelical Christian he wouldn't recommend conducting the survey. Many of the responses were Christians were anti-abortion, or anti-pornography, or anti-something. Some mentioned prominent conservative Christian leaders they had heard of, but none of the people he talked to said the term made them think of someone gracious or loving.

These days being called a Christian in many areas of this country, let alone the world is essentially the equivalent of being called a bad name. Christians are resented, feared, and avoided by large segments of our society, and the sad thing is, that in many ways it's understandable.

There are Christians who are judgmental, opinionated, stand offish, and bigoted. Some are unkind, selfish, rude, and snobbish. Even worse, there are some that are lazy, some liars, some cheat on on their taxes, and some are adulterers.

In short, name just about any negative attribute a human being can have and the chances are that I can find a "Christian" that has it. It's sad but true. The problem (not the excuse) is we are HUMAN! The fact we are all human is why my friend Jesus came to know me in the first place. He knew as a human that I had weaknesses, faults, and I just was not going to be able to make it as a <u>good</u> guy, and He came to *"save"* me!

Now I am not going into what he saved me from just yet. The purpose of this book is two fold. If you don't have a *"personal relationship"* with my friend Jesus, then I would encourage you to take the time to meet Him. Look past all of the brouhaha and falderal that complicates Christianity today and just meet Him. I trust He will take care of the rest.

The second purpose of this book is for those of you who have a *"personal relationship"* with our friend Jesus. Try to use this book as a mirror to see if you haven't let some of the things we are going to talk about creep into your "noble" efforts to introduce Jesus to others. And see, if maybe, just maybe, we can't all try to simplify things a bit. Let's see!

Chapter 1: Faith or Fiction

John 3:16(NIV)
"For God so loved the world that He gave His one and only Son that whoever believes in Him should not perish but have eternal life."

Some of you who do not have a personal relationship with my friend Jesus, are probably hung up on a couple of points already. For instance, in the verse I have quoted above I am asking you to take seriously the idea that some dead guy, who has been dead for over 2000 years can give you eternal life. That's impossible right from the start, isn't it?

Well there are many who feel logically and scientifically, you would be right. But on the other hand, there have been many, many things that were once thought to be impossible by logic or science that have since proven to be quite possible and logical.

One for instance, is the idea man can fly. The dream of a man being able to fly is as old as the story of Icarus, who flew too close to the sun. Leonardo De Vinci drew diagrams of flying machines, but as recently as the end of the 19th century, it was thought it was impossible for a man to fly. Similar ideas such as H. G. Wells' submarine and trip to the moon were considered nothing but science fiction until the 20th century.

I have to admit that every time that I get on an airplane, I have to suspend my sense of logic that something as heavy as a Boeing 747 jumbo jet can actual fly through thin air. Even, after studying the principles of flying, when I'm up there, it still seems impossible. However, I have faith in the people who have designed the plane and in the people that are flying it.

Isn't that really what faith is all about? It's putting our trust in someone enough so we will act on that trust even in situations we don't understand or that we can't logically explain. I have faith in pilots and planes. There is reasonable evidence and proof that these giant planes and their pilots are reliable. There is also reasonable evidence and proof that this Jesus of the Bible is reliable, worthy of my faith and trust.

You may feel it's impossible or illogical to believe that Jesus is who He says he is or did what the Bible says He did, but there are many very qualified scientists who believe that very thing.

One famous author, Josh McDowell, started a project many years ago to prove the Bible was basically fiction. He did a very careful and thorough study of not only what was in the Bible, but other historical records that were made at the time. He looked at every aspect you can imagine, and when he was done he had decided to formed a personal relationship with my friend Jesus, and wrote a very logical and scientific book called, "*Evidence that Demands a Verdict*".

Every year new things are being discovered and old ideas are being refuted. What was impossible yesterday, is possible today, and even scientists would agree what is impossible today may be very possible tomorrow

So I would like to request that for just a minute that you ask yourself a simple question:

"If it were possible for me to have the opportunity to be able to live forever, and someone had the power of giving it to me would I take it?"

While you are chewing on that question, let's add that not only would you live forever, but also you would be free of pain and suffering, your every need would be met. There would be no war or poverty, or disease. Wouldn't that be wonderful? Well, wouldn't it?

Now, if you have said yes to the question above, ask yourself what you would be willing to pay to have this opportunity? Would it be worth a million dollars, or a billion? Think about it. Rent free lodging for an unlimited amount of time without having to worry about where the next meal will come from, or whether the landlord is going to kick you out. How much would it be worth?

What if I told you it was free? Wouldn't you snap up the opportunity in an instant? Come on! Be honest, if you really thought it was possible, wouldn't you do it. What could you possibly have to lose?

That is exactly what my friend Jesus has offered you. **However,** there are two qualifications you need to have in order to be eligible for this deal.

Now I know that some of you are saying to yourself, just as you thought, there's a catch. You are probably thinking as good as this sounds, there is no such thing as a free ride. Well, in a way you're right. You definitely have to qualify for this offer. In fact there are two qualifications. Let's start by looking at the first.

Chapter 2: Who is the <u>Who</u> in Whoever?

John 3:16(NIV)
"For God so loved the world that He gave His one and only Son that whoever believes in Him should not perish but have eternal life."

Who is the <u>who</u> in "whoever"? That's the question that I would like to discuss in this chapter.

The verse above, "For God so loved the world that He gave His one and only Son that <u>whoever</u> believes in Him should not perish, but have eternal life." The first qualification is, you need to be a <u>who</u> in the "whoever". So you now might say, "Who does 'whoever' include?"

Does it include people of all ages? Does it include Whites, Blacks, Orientals, Hispanics or any other race? Does it include Catholics, Baptists, Jews, Mormons and Jehovah Witnesses? How about Muslims, Hindus, and Buddhists? What about atheists or agnostics? Or what about Ku Klux Klansmen?

Does it include heterosexuals, homosexuals, transsexuals, bisexuals, and transvestites?

Does it include liars, or adulterers, or people who cheat on their taxes?

Does it include, doctors, teachers, factory workers and lawyers, or even politicians?

Now we're getting a little tougher. Let's keep going anyway. Does it include criminals, even murderers and rapists?

Now let's get to the real tough questions. Does "whoever" include people who tell you with all sincerity they have a personal relationship with Jesus and they still lie, cheat, commit adultery, and maybe even murder and rape?

But the most important question of all is, does it include you?

The answer to all of these questions is a resounding **yes**!! "Whoever" includes everybody? Yes, that's right, everybody, good, bad, right or wrong! No matter how unworthy you think you are. No matter, what bad things you might have done. No matter what race, religion, or age group you fall under. Even if you think you don't need Jesus, or you are too intelligent to get caught up in this silliness, you are still a who in the "whoever"!

So the first of the two qualifications is a gimme. We all qualify! The second qualification is a different story. The second qualification requires an action on your part. In order to receive what Jesus is offering you need to **believe** in Him. Notice that this is a present tense verb. It means **believe** in Him now, not just acknowledging that He was a real person who lived a long time a go and died. It means we need to believe (have faith) and trust in a person that exists today.

There's that word faith again. Webster's dictionary defines faith as, "believing without proof, trust, or confidence. Imagine that, believing in something with out proof. That wouldn't make much sense would it? Yet we watch, "live television" and we believe that every thing that we are watching, even halfway across the world is absolutely true. Why? Because we have faith that the people that are producing the program are honest and the system that regulates television is reliable.

So the second qualification for the offer of eternal life is that you have to have faith that this Jesus who up until now you thought was dead and buried, or maybe wasn't a real person at all, is who He says He is, and that He did what He said He did. For some of you that may be harder than believing we can watch what's going on halfway across the world the instant that it's happening

With that in mind we are going to spend the rest of this book trying to make believing a little easier for you. In order to do that, I would like to use the next three chapters to try to strip away some of the obstacles that may result in making it harder for you to become a qualified believer.

Chapter 3: Lose the labels

1 Corinthians 13:4 (NIV)
"Love is patient, love is kind. It does not envy, it does not boast, it is not proud"

Labels are an important part of every day life. Practically everything that we buy today has a label on it, and in many cases law requires them. We use labels to help us determine whether the item we are trying to purchase is really what we are looking for.

Labels are used to tell us a wide variety of things about what we are looking to purchase including size, weight, brand, and ingredients. Take soup for instance, if you have gone down the aisle in the grocery store where they sell soup recently you can see a practically endless supply of varieties and flavors. There are as many as a dozen different chicken variations alone. Now if you include the beef, vegetable, and seafood variations as well, the choices are formidable.

Imagine if you would walk down that aisle tomorrow and every single can on the shelf said just one word, SOUP! What would you do? You would have no idea what was in any particular can unless you would actually have to open it, look at it, and taste it. You certainly couldn't make any assumptions about it otherwise.

Don't we make those types of assumptions about people however? If I would tell you that I am a liberal, or a conservative, a Republican, or a Democrat, an environmentalist, or a capitalist you would probably form a fairly defined opinion of me on the spot.

Now you may be thinking that you are not that way. If so, let's try an example. If I would walk up to you on the street and tell you I am an alcoholic what would you think of me? Now let's imagine I came up to you and said I am a recovering alcoholic, and I haven't had a drop of alcohol in ten years, I am also an independent business man who employees 35 people in the local community, and I am a member of the school board, would your opinion of me change? Be honest, would it?

It's like that with every label we plaster on each other. Christians, included. The words liberal, conservative, evangelical, fundamentalist, charismatic, etc often cause us to have a immediate opinion about a person, but in reality just like the different cans of soup, there are many different types of Christians. We don't all come from the same pot.

The verse I quoted at the beginning of the chapter tells us loving other people means being, patient, and kind. I believe every time we make a snap judgment about someone based on one of these labels we are failing the litmus test for being loving.

Now I don't want you to confuse what I am saying with being politically correct. I firmly believe that truth is truth and correct is correct. Politically correct means to me that I am going to do something or say something, or not do something, or say something based upon what impact it will have on my personal popularity.

I believe the reason that we are told, to love means to be patient, kind, not envious or proud, is because it's the right thing to do no matter what impact is has on me personally. Jesus spent a lot of time with lepers, prostitutes, and tax gatherers. These were not the type of people who could get you ahead politically, either during Jesus' time or today.

He spent time with them because He loved them. Just like you can't decide what's in a label less can of soup without opening it. We can't decide to reject someone without taking the time to get to know them. Including my friend Jesus.

For now, as you read this book, let's try to set labels aside and get down to the basics. What is a Christian really? I would like to define a Christian as someone who has a personal relationship with Jesus Christ. Simple as that. Once you establish you want to be a Christian, you can have the fun of deciding how to fill out the rest of the label on your can, but just like you can't be "Chicken Soup", if you're not soup first. You can't define who you are as a Christian until you decide to become one first.

So don't reject the idea of having a personal relationship with Jesus because of any preconceived ideas you might have of what a Christian is, or should be.

Chapter 4: Junk the Jargon

1 Corinthians 14:9

"Unless you speak intelligible words with your tongue how will anyone Know what you are saying?"

The English language is one of the hardest languages to learn. We have so many synonyms and homonyms and multiples uses for the same word that many times you can't define a word until you hear it in a sentence.

There is a famous Russian comedian Yakov Smirnoff who has made a very popular comedy routine out of how confusing our language can be. One of his examples is: *"America is the only country where you park on a driveway and drive on a parkway. What a country!"*

One of our friends was telling about a new employee they have at work who is from China. He and his co-workers are trying to teach this poor guy some of our more popular idioms each week. Phrases like, "look what the cat dragged in", or "it's better than a poke in the eye with a sharp stick". Who thinks these things up anyway?

Different industries have their own terminology as well. I have a consulting business in the communications industry and often times our terminology looks like alphabet soup. We talk about PBXs, and CCS, IP Technology, DID numbers and ARS, just to name a few. One of my services that I provide to my clients is that I try to translate some of the "jargon" into terms they can understand. I often say I know several languages, such as AT&T, Verizon, and MCI.

Even quilters have their own terminology. My wife, Laura has been getting more and more interested in quilting over the last year, and she watches a quilting show each day. Sometimes I listen in and it seems as if they have invented their own language. They talk about biases, swatches, rotary cutters, feed dogs, walking feet, and long arm quilting machines. You could get nightmares from some of those terms!

One term in particular got my attention. Every quilter who has been quilting for any length of time starts to collect pile after pile of material. Often times they will buy a piece of material because they like the style or color, even when they don't have a quilt right now to put it in. This collection of material is referred to as the quilter's "stash". Well the first time she referred to her "stash" around some twenty-something people that we knew she got quite a look, because the word stash has other meanings in today's society.

This type of thing makes for funny conversations some times, but the bottom line is if we don't understand someone else's terminology it can make it pretty hard to communicate.

Unfortunately, Christians are often guilty of using terminology just as confusing. Words such as sanctification, apologetics, redemption, and charismatic are not part of every day language for most of us and our definition for these words may not even be the same for every person that uses them.

In addition some of the phrases we use can be confusing and maybe even frightening. Imagine a young couple entering a church for the first time and having a big burly guy in a plaid sport coat come up to them and shake their hand and ask them if they have been baptized in the blood of Jesus Christ! Other terms like have you been born again, or have you been redeemed by the cross may seem very clear to a Christian, but to someone who has never held a Bible in their hand, (like a young man that I met a few weeks ago told me), the words aren't clear at all. As much as possible I think we need to take the advice of Paul in his first letter to the Corinthians, which I quoted at the beginning of this chapter. "Unless you speak intelligible words with your tongue, how will anyone know what you are saying?"

As a result I would like to make two suggestions. First if you are a Christian, I would urge you to make sure that when you talk to friends and family about our friend Jesus that you try very hard to use terminology that's easy for them to understand.

Even our illustrations need to be clear. During the time Jesus was teaching, He often used a story or "parable" to illustrate what He was trying to say. The subjects of His stories were very familiar to the people He was telling them to.

One such story is about the "Good Shepherd." In this story Jesus refers to Himself as the "gate", saying; "Whoever enters through me will be saved" The people listening to Jesus knew exactly what Jesus was talking about, because sometimes the shepherds of the time would herd their sheep into an enclosed area like a cave or grove of trees and then lie down at the entrance to sleep. Literally the shepherd became the gate to the pen. The shepherd then protected the sheep that entered into the area.

Stories and illustrations like this can still be very helpful in explaining what it means to have a relationship with Jesus Christ, but if you are using a story with a friend or family member, make sure that they understand what the story is about, especially stories from the Bible.

My second suggestion is, if you don't have a personal relationship with my friend Jesus and some one tries to talk to you about Him, and they use a word or expression you don't understand, stop them and ask them to explain what that term or expression means.

After all, if they are trying to share with you about some thing that may affect you not just today, or tomorrow, or next year, but for eternity, then I think that you have a right to have a clear understanding of what it is all about

For the last few years my wife and I have been involved in a jail ministry in our community and one of the other guys in the ministry named Bob, has a real sensitivity for this issue, and often when someone is giving a sermon he will stop them in mid-sentence and ask them to explain a term they are using. Now to some people that may seem rude, but we are there in order to help introduce people to Jesus, and for Bob, that means it's important they know what we're talking about!

That's important in this book as well. My business is communication, and if two people are talking and one doesn't understand the other, then communication doesn't exist. As we discussed earlier, my purpose is to make it as easy as possible for people to meet Jesus, so as much as possible let's "junk the jargon". So I am going to try to stay away from "Christian" terminology and expressions and try to stick with just plain English. After all, that's hard enough to understand by itself isn't it?

Chapter 5: Dump the Denominations

Acts 11:26

"The disciples were called Christians first at Antioch"

I live in a medium sized city in northern Indiana. The population of the city is about 12,000. If I look in the telephone book under churches, the yellow pages give me 39 different categories or *"denominations"* of churches. There are actually five different categories of Baptist churches alone. Besides the Baptist denomination, there are Assemblies of God, Catholic, Lutheran, United Methodist, Missionary, Nazarene, Seventh-day Adventist, Grace Brethren, Brethren, etc.

Is it any wonder then it's confusing to know what it means to be a Christian, if there are 39 different choices of *"Christian"* churches in one community alone?

The purpose of this chapter is not to try to explain the differences between these different denominations. It would take someone a lot more qualified than I to try to do that, and a lot larger book. In fact, to tell the truth, I haven't got the slightest idea of what the difference is between an Independent Baptist, a Southern Baptist, and a Regular Baptist church.

Even though I am sure that I am going to take a little heat for saying this, the purpose of this chapter is to encourage you to look past or even ignore the different denominations as you make your decision to meet Jesus Christ and believe in him.

Now, I am not saying that any particular denomination is bad, but if having so many choices is making it harder for you, or any one else to make a decision to have a personal relationship with my friend Jesus, then I think they are not helping.

With the risk of putting myself in hot water again, I would like to say I don't believe it was Jesus' intention to have all of these deominations exist today. Jesus told the people He had come to save sinners, not Lutherans, Methodists, or Presbyterians.

Webster's dictionary defines the word denomination as a religious group or sect. By definition a group is made up of people, and I believe that people are responsible for denominations, not Jesus. In this same dictionary, there is a relevant quote by two men Ogburn and Nimkoff. They say, "The presence of many different denominations and sects in a society means that the culture is differentiated into many parts, with differing group interests and viewpoints." I think that this statement is true. Denominations exist because people differ in their viewpoints of what they believe that their church should be. As the result of these differences, divisions occur and denominations appear.

In many cases these differences are for important reasons and the splits that occurred may be necessary. In other cases the differences may be quite unimportant in the eyes of God. I am not trying to make judgments as to which ones were good and which ones were bad, because I am neither knowledgeable or qualified enough to do that.

The bottom line is that when it comes to meeting Jesus Christ and determining whether or not you want to have a personal relationship with Him all 39 different denominations in my telephone book do not matter. Jesus has made it possible for you to become a believer in Him and receive His free gift of eternal life without picking the "right" denomination.

There are many people who have been discouraged with making even an effort to meet Jesus Christ. The idea of determining what Church is the right Church is just too confusing. How can Jesus be the *one* way to heaven if all these people have so many different ideas?

The answer to that question is that there is only one person who has promised to provide you the gift of eternal life. Then he backed it up in every way possible, even being raised from the dead. This person is Jesus Christ! If you are to receive the gift He has promised you, it will only be through your faith in Him, and His ability to be wholly deserving of that faith. Membership in a church does not earn anyone, anything.

On the flip side of the coin for all of the people who have been discouraged from meeting Jesus Christ because of confusion over which Church is the "right" Church, there are even more today who have not taken the step of entering into that relationship because they believe they are "safe" because they believe they do belong to the "right" Church.

I know this is true because that is exactly the way I felt for the first 24 years of my life. I was born and raised in a particular denomination of church and was taught that being born into that denomination and participating by following their rules and regulations was what I needed to do to obtain eternal life. This church taught me all about Jesus, and what He had done in dying on the cross. The one thing that I didn't learn is that I needed to make a *personal* commitment to Jesus.

When I was 24 years old I met someone who introduced me to Jesus in a whole new way. Growing up, I had never been encouraged to read the Bible for myself. When I did, I realized that Jesus had died specifically for me! Not exclusively for me, but specifically for me! It was then that I decided to put the responsibility for my salvation totally in His hands, and not in mine or my church's.

To all of you people who are like me and were brought up with the idea that if you were born into a particular church or denomination you are "*saved*" I would also encourage you to "dump the denominations". Membership in a church alone is not a qualification for salvation. A relationship with Jesus Christ qualifies us to be a member of His church not the other way around.

In the verse that I quoted at the beginning of this chapter, "The disciples were called Christians first at Antioch"(Acts 11:26). The disciples were called Christians, because they had made a commitment to Jesus Christ, not a church! In fact, going to a church each week, or even being a member of a particular church, although it may be helpful in enabling you to learn about Jesus or His Father, is no more necessary to your salvation than having a library card. Both are excellent places to learn, but just sitting in them doesn't do you any good.

Don't get me wrong! In no way am I discouraging anyone from attending church regularly becoming involved in a church family or becoming a member. All I am saying is don't confuse going to church with having a relationship with Jesus Christ!

Having a relationship with Jesus Christ is a lot more personal and a lot more intimate than just sitting in church on Sunday. It takes a day-to-day, week-to-week, year-to-year commitment. But isn't that the same with any worthwhile relationship?

So, how exactly do you meet my friend Jesus and find out what you need to do to enter into a personal relationship with Him? Well, the first step is to look in the mirror and meet yourself.

Chapter 6: See Your Self

Romans 3:23

"For all have sinned and fall short of the glory of God"

Mirror, mirror, on the wall, who's the fairest one of all? I am sure that just about all of us are familiar with this line from the fairy tale Snow White. The evil queen starts off each day by asking the magic mirror this same question, and each day the mirror comes back and shows the queen her reflection and proceeds to tell her she is the fairest of them all.

Each day she knows that of all the people in the land she sets the standard for beauty. Then one day she gets up and looks in the mirror and asks the question and instead of her reflection she sees Snow White, and she is no longer the standard! She is no longer the best! She is still beautiful, but that's not good enough for her and we all know the rest of the story.

You know I wonder what it would be like to have a magic mirror like that and to be able to look into it and ask a different question. I wonder whose reflection the mirror would show if we asked it; Mirror, mirror on the wall, who is the most perfect one of all. Would it be yours? I know it wouldn't be mine. I think just about all of us would probably agree that we're not perfect. In fact the saying nobody's perfect is an excuse we often hear when someone forgets something or makes a mistake. Nobody's perfect!

It's kind of funny that we are all pretty comfortable with not being perfect, but many of us have a hard time admitting that we are a *sinner*. Webster's Dictionary defines sin as breaking a law of God, wrongdoing of any kind, whether an immoral act, lying, stealing, dishonesty, or cruelty. That's a pretty broad base to work with and yet we are still hesitant to say that we are sinners.

A recent survey of the American population revealed about 80 percent of the people believe there is a heaven, and almost as great a percentage believe they are going to go there.

When asked why they think they are going to heaven a large percentage of them gave an answer based upon what in school we would call grading on a curve. They gave answers like:

"Well I'm better than most people"
"I've never done anything really bad"
"I'm not a criminal or anything"
"Overall I'm not that bad"

The problem with an answer like this is; what is the standard and who gets to define it? How good is not that bad, and how do I know if it's good enough?

I think us saying we are good enough to get to heaven is something like me saying I am good enough to play professional football. I may define the standard any way I want, but when it comes down to reality I would be lucky to survive one play.

So how can we be so convinced we are going to heaven if we don't know how to determine if we qualify? Unlike the queen in Snow White, we don't know who to compare ourselves to in order to find out whether we make the grade.

Or do we? There is only one human being in history whose character has been described as perfect, Jesus. The Bible says in Hebrews 4:15, "but we have one who was tempted in every way, just as we are, yet was without sin." I believe if we had a magic mirror on the wall and we asked it to reveal the most perfect person it would reveal Jesus. So just like Snow White was the standard for beauty, Jesus is the standard for perfection.

So where does that leave us? Well, it leaves us short of the standard. The verse I used at the beginning of this chapter is Romans 3:23 "For all have sinned and fall short of the glory of God". We all fall short.

So if we all fall short where does that leave the person who is better than most people? Not good enough. Where does it leave the person who's not a criminal? Not good enough. Where does it leave me? Where does it leave you? Not good enough.

Quite a few years ago there was as daredevil motorcycle rider who said that he could jump a large canyon in Colorado called the Snake River Canyon on his rocket powered motorcycle. This daredevil had tried a number of other stunts and had been successful, so when he made this claim the media made a big thing about it and his attempt was televised on national television.

When it was the time to make the jump his rocket powered cycle took off from one side of the canyon and flew about a third of the way across before it started to take a nosedive and the rider had to parachute to safety. The fact of the matter was he didn't even come close.

It appeared that the only way that his motorcycle could make it from one side of that canyon to the other was if someone built a bridge and he rode it across.

Just like this daredevil there are many, many people who are risking their lives, not just their present lives, but their eternal lives trying to prove they are good enough to jump the gap between themselves and God. The problem is no matter how good they are they will always fall short.

Just like that rider they need a bridge, and God provided that bridge in Jesus. Romans 5:8 says; "While we were yet sinners Christ died for us".

So, if you look in the mirror, not a magic mirror, but just any mirror, you will see an imperfect person in need of help. Help to cross the bridge. Don't feel bad; we all see the same thing.

So if you are one of the 80 percent of the population that believes there is a heaven and then by definition a hell as well, then maybe it's time to ask for some help. If you are one of the 20 percent who would say no, there is no heaven, then you need to ask yourself another question. What if I am wrong?

I had a friend who was an atheist and he and I would have some glorious debates about God, and sin, heaven and hell, Jesus and salvation. We would go around and around for hours. Then one day he was going to move away to take a new job in another state and I had one more chance to talk to him because for whatever reason I was sure I wouldn't ever see him again.

I remember saying to him that night. If you are right and I am wrong then we are both going to end up as worm food. Dust for dust, and dirt for dirt. But if I'm right and you're wrong then you are going to be in a whole lot of trouble. I asked him if he really was that big of a risk taker.

That's the way we left it, and to this day I don't know if his opinion has changed, but I know mine has not. I am not willing to take that kind of chance, are you?

Maybe it's time to meet Jesus, just meet Him, and see if maybe He has something to offer you that you are not willing to refuse. Maybe it's time to meet the Master.

Chapter 7: Meet The Master

John 14:6

"Jesus answered, "I am the way and the truth and the life. No one comes to the Father except through me. If you really knew me you would know my Father as well."

At the beginning of the book I said one of its purposes was to try to encourage you to meet my friend Jesus. Well hopefully if you are still reading you are ready to do that. The next question then is "how do you meet Jesus"?

Let me start out by saying it's not hard to meet Jesus, because He really wants you to! In the verse above Jesus says that if you really knew Him you would know His Father and His Father is God. Jesus wants you to know Him and His Father.

Why? Because He loves you! The whole reason He lived and the reason He died and the reason for Him being raised from the dead was He loves you and wants you to enter into an eternal relationship with Him. Now I don't know about you, but given how I act sometimes someone really has to like me to want to spend any time with me at all. How much would someone have to love you to want to spend eternity with you?

So if Jesus wants us to meet Him, how do we do that? Well in today's world there are a variety of ways to meet people. We can meet them in person, we can write them a letter, we can call them on the phone, we can chat with them in a chat room, we can even make eye contact with them across a crowded room. But in all of these ways there has to be communication verbal, written, non-verbal communication.

Jesus has provided us with ways to communicate with Him. One way is through the Bible. As a Christian I believe that the Bible is the Word of God, which means simply that when we read it, it's God talking to us. Now for some of you that may be a stretch, but I believe the case for it is very strong. There is a reason there have been more Bibles printed than any other book. Skeptics tried to prove it's content wrong over the years, but none of it has been refuted.

However the purpose of this book is not to prove that the Bible is God's personal communication to us, it's only to encourage you to read it and decide for yourself. So where do you start?

I believe everything in the Bible has merit, and it's all worth reading. In fact I would encourage you to make it a goal to read it through cover-to-cover. However, to begin with, since I wanted to introduce you to Jesus, I think it would be best to start with the books that tell about Jesus' life. These books are called the *Gospels*, which means "Good News" Mathew Mark, Luke and John are narrative eye-witness accounts of the life of Jesus.. Of the four I would recommend starting with the book of John, and then read the other three in any order you wish. From there you could read the rest of the *New Testament*, a term for the books written after Jesus' birth.

Now there are several translations of the Bible and it's important to choose one that will make it as easy as possible for you to learn about Jesus. There are a lot of good translations that are translated directly from the original writings, but two that I would recommend are the New International Version and the New Living Bible. This is not to say that other translations like the New American Standard, or the King James Version are not good sources, but I believe the two that I am recommending are written in more contemporary language. As I mention earlier in the book, if two people are exchanging information and one doesn't understand the other then communication does not exist. If I wrote this book in German, it would only make sense to someone who reads German. Reading the Bible won't do you any good if you can't understand it!

So one way to meet Jesus is to read the Bible. Another way is by talking to people who know Him. Now if you wanted to meet me you might say that it would make more sense to just go and talk to me, however, by knowing what kind of friends I have and what they think about me you can find out a lot about me and get to know me pretty well.

I would imagine that if you are reading this book you might know someone who describes himself as a Christian. I would encourage you to talk to that person and be sure to ask them questions about Jesus. You might want to let them know you don't expect them to have all of the answers, because they probably won't, but you might start with asking them how they met Jesus.

I would also encourage you to go to church. One way that we can get to know Jesus is by going to His house and meeting His family. That's what we are when we become Christians, brothers and sisters of Jesus. There are a lot of different churches and I'm not going to recommend one in particular; however I would strongly recommend that you go to a church that teaches that the Bible is God's Word and that it is the basis for their beliefs.

One thing I would caution you about is that even though we are part of Jesus' family, we are not Jesus. When we enter into a relationship with Jesus it's with the understanding that we were and we are sinners, and we need Him. So even though as Christians we may reflect Jesus' character, it's like going to the carnival and looking in the mirror at the fun house, it's distorted. As Christians we try to reflect Jesus, but it's distorted by our sin.

The final way we can meet Jesus is simply by talking to Him. That's what is known as *prayer*. Prayer is having a conversation with Jesus. I imagine some of you are thinking well, how does He hear me? Do I have to pray out loud? Do I have to be in church? Do I have to pray a certain way? The answer is just talk to Him. Talk to Him like you would talk to someone that you wanted to get to know.

Be honest; tell Him how you really feel, tell Him the good and the bad. Jesus is the one person who knows us better than anyone else and still loves us. We can tell Him what is really troubling us and put it in His hands. We can also trust Him. The Bible says there was no deception in Him, and He promises He will never leave us or forsake us. So take a chance, just talk to Him!

Now for those of you who are skeptics, you are probably thinking I can talk until I'm blue in the face but no one is going to hear me, because no one is there. I am not going to try to explain to you how prayer works, but I can testify by experience that it does. We live in a world that is full of information, literally full of it. As I mentioned earlier in the book, I work in the field of communication and what's amazing to me is the amount information that surrounds us every minute of the day. We literally travel through information. Information flows through the air, on radio waves, light waves, micro waves, cellular waves, satellite waves and laser beams. We are practically drowning in it.

We can pick up our cellular phone and tap a couple of buttons and ring another phone clear across the world. We can get on our computer, type a message, and in seconds we get a response back from someone in a place we don't even know. A reporter can set up a satellite feed and send live pictures of events that are happening all around the globe. All of these phenomenons are the inventions of human beings, and I can't even begin to tell you how they all work, but they do.

With all of this in mind, if man can accomplish this, what do you suppose the God who created the universe could do? I believe hearing you pray to Him would be a pretty simple feat to Him, and it is.

When we pray to Jesus, He does hear us and the Bible tells us He will answer us. Now exactly how He will answer you, I can't tell you. God spoke to Moses from a burning bush. He spoke to others through dreams, and to some He spoke through other people called *prophets*. Jesus spoke to Paul on the road to Damascus after He struck Him blind. The best advice I can give you is to just talk to Him and then listen.

So that's it! It may sound simple, because it is. Jesus is just waiting to meet you and after you have, He will change your life. How do I know? Because He has changed mine.

In a court of law, in order to a prove a point, a lawyer may call witnesses to come forward and provide testimony as to whether or not a certain aspect of their case is true. In the *court of eternity*, God has called those of us who call themselves by His name, Christians, to be willing to provide our testimony on His behalf. So in the next chapter I would ask you to test my testimony.

Chapter 8: Test the Testimony

Philippians 4: 6,7

"Do not be anxious about anything, but in everything by prayer and petition, with thanksgiving, present your requests to God. And the peace of God which transcends all understanding, will guard your hearts and minds in Christ Jesus"

This chapter is my testimony about the change that a personal relationship with Jesus Christ has made in my life. I present it to you as evidence as to why I believe it is so important for you to have a relationship with Him as well.

Probably the best way to sum up the difference in my life before I entered into a personal relationship with Jesus and my life since could best be summed up in one word: Peace! The kind of peace Paul talks about in the verses I have quoted at the beginning of this chapter, the kind of peace that surpasses understanding.

This peace has characterized itself in a couple of different ways. First of all, it has given me peace about what will happen to me when I die. Prior to entering into my relationship with Jesus, I believed in hell, and I believed it was definitely a place, and a place where I didn't want to end up.

However, that's where I thought I was headed, and it scared me, pardon the pun, to death. I knew the difference between right and wrong, but I wasn't able to end up consistently on the right side, and as a result I was afraid of what would happen if I died.

Now just so you know, if I didn't believe in hell, and thought what would happened when I die was that I would just cease to be, I think that would have scared me just as much, so suffice to say, fear was a real factor in my life.

When I entered into my relationship with Jesus, and trusted the fact that His death on the cross paid the penalty for my sins, and His resurrection sealed my place with Him for eternity, my fear simply went away. The day that I asked Jesus to become a very real part of my life, I remember that my overwhelming emotion was one of relief. I wasn't scared to die anymore.

In fact, I can honestly still say that today 27 years later, and a lot closer to the end of my life now then I was back then. While I am not wild about the idea of dying, and all of the pain and suffering that can go along with it, and I am not looking forward to leaving my loved ones behind, death itself does not scare me. This is a very real and enormous difference from the way I was before.

The second area in which I have experienced the peace Paul describes has been in my daily life. One thing I found out after I became a Christian is that Jesus wanted me to trust Him for more than just my salvation. He wanted me to trust Him with my life.

After I entered into a relationship with Jesus, He sent His Spirit to become a very real part of my life. In chapter 14, verse 26, of the book of John, Jesus tells the disciples "But the Counselor, the Holy Spirit will teach you all things and will remind you of everything that I have said to you." Now I am not talking about a visit from the ghost of Jacob Marley or the ghost of Christmas yet to come, but I am talking about a real communication I now have with God that I didn't have before.

The best analogy I can come up with to explain it to you is by comparing it to football.

Before I begin, I need to let you know I am a big football fan. In fact many of my friends, including my wife would call me a big football fanatic, and I do have to admit during the professional football season my favorite television channel is the NFL Network, so for me this analogy is perfect.

However, if you are not a big football fan, it may not be as perfect for you, so I will try to explain it and I hope it helps.

First of all, for many years the person who was responsible for calling plays for a football team was the quarterback. During the week he and his coaches would work on what they called a game plan, which was their best guess of what plays would work that week against the team they were playing. It would provide guidelines to the quarterback as to what would be the best plays to call. However when the game started, it was up to the quarterback to call the right play. This put a lot of pressure on one man, and because of that, the best quarterbacks weren't always the best athletes, but they were the ones who could best make these kinds of decisions under pressure. After all, if the quarterback called the wrong play he was responsible for the result.

Technology has improved in today's football world. The quarterback is no longer the one who is calling the plays. The quarterbacks actually have microphones and radio receivers in their helmets and the plays are relayed to the quarterback from a coach who sits in the television booth.

This coach has a lot of advantages the quarterback doesn't. From his spot in the booth he can see the whole field and he can tell where all of the defensive players are located. He also has a computer which gives him all of the other teams statistics and tendencies at his finger tips, Television monitors allow him to replay previous plays and produce still pictures of the defensive team so that he can analyze what they're doing. As of a result of all of this technology, the coach is in a lot better position to call the plays than the quarterback. Now the quarterback still has the ability to change or not call the play the coach gives him, but when he does, if the play doesn't work, then he really has to take the heat.

How does this relate to my relationship with Jesus and the Holy Spirit? Before I entered into a personal relationship with Jesus I was like the old time quarterback. I had the Bible, and I believed in it, and that was my game plan. However, when I started reacting to the realities of life and the problems that I faced, I was basically calling the shots from my very limited perspective. Sometimes I called the right play, and sometimes I didn't and the game plan was often set aside.

After I entered into a relationship with Jesus, I gave Him the responsibility for calling the plays for my life and the Holy Spirit became my receiver. This allowed Him to communicate with me. The advantages were obvious. You can imagine if the football coach has a lot better perspective to call the plays from the booth, how much better is God's perspective to call the plays for your life when He knows you better than anyone and also loves you more than anyone.

Now I was not immediately convinced. Pride stood in the way of me completely surrendering the responsibility for God to direct my life. However I found the more I allowed the Spirit to direct me, the better I felt, about my life, and about myself, and the more "peace" I had. Just as in football, when a quarterback and coach have been working together for a number of years, they start thinking alike and working better together, I found myself thinking more and more like I feel

Jesus would, and finding out that He and I were "on the same page".

Also, just as in football, when a quarterback has had success listening to a particular coach he tends to trust him faster and more often, the same has been for my relationship with Jesus. As I have experienced the success of working with Him in my life, I have begun to trust Him more and more and my confidence in Him has grown.

I want you to know I am not saying if you enter into a relationship with Jesus everything will be roses and lollipops. Some of the most difficult situations I have had to face have come during my times as a Christian.

I was fired from a very secure job; my first wife divorced me, and gave me the responsibility for raising my nine-year-old son. My mother died at a relatively young age after a long and very difficult illness. However during every difficulty that I have faced over the last 27 years God has been faithful and I can say with conviction I have always felt His presence, in the best of times and in the worst of times.

The very best testimony I can give for the benefits of a relationship with Jesus is; I would never, under any circumstances want to go back to the way my life was before I personally met Jesus. You couldn't make me, or pay me enough to give up the peace I now have for the chaos I had then.

So, how about you? I want you to have the same peace I have, and I hope that you want that too. When I started the book I said there were two qualifications you needed to enter into a relationship with Jesus. One you have by default in that you are a "who" in the whoever. The second qualification is that you need to believe in Jesus.

Now it's time to find out what you need to do to be a believer!

Chapter 9: Be a Believer

Romans 10: 9-10

"That if you confess with your mouth, "Jesus is Lord," and believe in your heart that God raised Him from the dead, you will be saved. For it is with your heart that you believe and are justified and it is with your mouth that you confess and are saved."

If you are still reading this book at this point, I hope when you are done you will find a Bible and read the book of John and start meeting my friend Jesus. Once you have done that I am confident you will want to make a relationship with Him a very real part of your life. So you will probably want to know how to do that. How do you become a qualified believer as described in John 3:16?

The verses I have quoted above lay it out quite clearly. You need to believe Jesus was who He said He was, and you have to declare Him as the Lord of your life. But, what does that mean?

First of all, who did Jesus say that He was? Well in John 14:6 Jesus said "I am the way and the truth and the life. No one comes to the Father except through me. If you really knew me you would know my Father as well. From now on you do know Him and have seen Him."

Jesus said He was the Son of God the Father, and God Himself, and the only way to the Father. In John 1: 1 it says, "In the beginning was the Word and the Word was with God and the Word was God. He was with God in the beginning." Then in John 1:14, John says, "The Word was made flesh and made His dwelling among us. We have seen His glory.

Then in John 1: 17-18, "For the law was given to Moses; grace and truth came through Jesus Christ. No one has ever seen God, but God the one and only, who is at the Father's side has made Him known."

So who does Jesus say He is? He is the Son of God the Father, He is God, He died on a cross as a sacrifice for our sins. He was resurrected from the dead after three days and He is only way to eternal life. That is what you need to believe!

Many people try to water down who Jesus said He was. They say that he was a good teacher, a prophet, or a good example of how to live our lives. It's not enough to believe that Jesus existed, that He lived and died, and He was a good man or you believe in what He taught. That will gain you nothing.

Believing Jesus was anything less than God, is like believing in a compass not pointing true north. It looks good on the outside, but if you follow it, you will get lost.

When I was in the Navy, I worked in the ship's Captains office for about nine months. That job gave me access to just about every part of the ship. One of my favorite places was the ship's bridge. This was the part of the ship where all the action was. They kept track of where we were, where we going, and everything around us and of course this is where the ship was steered from.

One of the things I was most impressed by was the ship's helm. It was a wheel about four feet in diameter and even though the ship I was on was a huge aircraft carrier, somehow the simple movement of that wheel could alter the direction of the ship.

Whenever we left port the helmsman was given a heading to follow. This heading was entered into a device that was attached to the helm and the helmsman had to keep a needle or arrow pointed on that heading as we traveled. Because of the rising and falling of the waves, and the weather conditions the needle was constantly moving first one way then the other, and the helmsman always had to bring it back on the heading.

The thing that amazed me the most was; if at the beginning of the day the helmsman started just one degree off from the heading and continued on that course for the whole day the ship could be as much as 100 miles off course. So far off course that in the ocean you would probably go right by your objective and miss it entirely. Just one little degree!

That's the way it is with the truth about Jesus. If you try to shade the truth one little degree, you miss the point entirely. The only way Jesus can accomplish everything He said He would is if He were God. He is either God, a liar or a lunatic, there is no middle ground. There is no gray area.

So in order to be a believer you have to believe Jesus was who He said He was, God, not just a God, but God, not just a son of God, but the only begotten Son of God.

Secondly you have to declare Him as the Lord of your life. What does that mean? Webster's dictionary defines the word lord as owner, ruler or master. That doesn't sound very friendly does it? You might be thinking right now when I started this book all I was asking was that you would meet my friend Jesus, and that He wants to be your friend too. Well that's true, but He wants to be more than that. He wants you to trust Him. To trust Him enough so you will allow Him to be responsible for not just your eternal life, but also your life here and now!

In medieval times, the lord of a town or city was responsible for the citizens of that town. It was his responsibility to make sure they were protected and provided for. The people counted on the lord to provide them what they couldn't provide for themselves. If the lord was kind and responsible the people were happy, taken care of and prospered. If the lord was evil and power hungry the people were oppressed and suffered. The key wasn't in the title but in the character of the man who held it.

That's the way it is with my friend Jesus. It is in His character we can put our trust! It is His desire to be there for you and help you to be the very best person you can be. He will be there for you in the good times, and He will be there for you in the hard times. In Hebrews 13: 6 God says "Never will I leave you; never will I forsake you."

Part of making him the Lord of your life is you have to turn away from your old life to make Him the Lord of your new life. That is what is called *"repentance"*. Now that doesn't mean that we have to quit being sinners before we can accept Jesus, because if it did, none of us would qualify.

To use the medieval analogy a bit further, if someone wanted to move into a city or town they were required to give up their allegiance to their old lord and swear allegiance to their new lord. That meant that they would no longer obey their old lord, but would obey the new.

That is what happens when we become Christians. We pledge allegiance to Jesus and pledge to turn our backs on our old way of life. The key is that even then or especially then, we still need help. That's what the Holy Spirits does. He helps us to be able to understand what in our lives we need to change and how to change them.

So in order to be a believer we have to believe Jesus is who He says He is and we have to make Him Lord of our life. Is that it? Well, not quite. The verse at the beginning of the chapter says that we have to declare with our mouths that Jesus is Lord. That means we have to make it known. You have to say it. Simply put, you need to admit that you are a sinner and that you want to turn away from your old life and you need Jesus, and just ask Him to be a real, and vital part of your life. Decide to let him take control of your game plan!

This may mean you call up your friend who wants you to be a Christian and tell them you took the big step. However, I believe Jesus wants us to be a little more specific. In Romans chapter 6: 3-4 Paul says "Or don't you know that all of us who were baptized into Christ Jesus were baptized into death in order that just as Christ was raised from the dead through the glory of the Father, we too may live a new life." This is where the term *"born again"* comes from. To be reborn into a new life as a Christian, symbolized by baptism.

In Mathew 28: 19 Jesus told His disciples before He left them "Therefore go and make disciples of all nations, baptizing them in the name of the Father, the Son and the Holy Spirit. Jesus told His disciples to baptize the new believers."

So I believe Jesus wants us to make a public declaration of the change that has come into our life, by taking the step of baptism.

Unfortunately in the world we live in, that's not always possible. In some parts of the world a declaration like this could result in being thrown out of a family, publicly ridiculed, arrested, or even executed.

God knows our hearts. He knows your heart. If you want to become a John 3:16 believer but the opportunity doesn't exist to make a public declaration of your faith then make a private declaration with a single friend or witness and pray He will change the circumstances in whatever way needed to allow you to make a bolder statement. Also it is not necessary to be baptized in a public ceremony by a minister if that's not possible. You can be baptized by another Christian in a bathtub or in a pond in the country just like the Ethiopian baptized by Philip in Acts 8: 36

You need to know that faith in Christ is a journey it starts with the first step. This is the first step! Be a believer! Reach out and take Jesus' hand and He will lead you on a journey you will never forget or regret. His is the hand you will never want to let go!

If you have come to the point where you have decided you want to make Jesus the Lord of your life there are some verses at the end of this book that will help you to make what we call a "confession of faith" and ask Jesus to enter into a new relationship with you!

I know that there are probably still some doubters among you who just haven't been convinced. That's okay. Convincing you is not my job! My job is just to testify to what I know is true.

However, I would be lying if I didn't admit that I would like to convince you, and excuse me for not understanding why I can't. But if you are like my engineering friend who loved to debate me, but wouldn't believe me, I would like to close this chapter with the words of the first verse and chorus of a song by a lovely young woman named Nicole Nordeman who uses the enormous talent that she has to tell people about **her** friend Jesus. The name of the song is "<u>What If</u>"

What If?

What if you're right?
And he was just another nice guy.
What if you're right?
What if it's true?
They say the cross will only make a fool of you.
And what if it's true?

What if he takes his place in history
With all the prophets and the kings
Who taught us love and came in peace,
But then the story ends
What then?

But what if you're wrong?
What if there's more?
What if there's hope you never dreamed of hoping for?
What if you just close your eyes?
What if the arms that catch you catch you by surprise?
What if He's more than enough?
What if it's love?

WHAT IF

Chapter 10: Forgive the Forgiven

Mark 2: 3-12

"Some men came bringing to him a paralytic, carried by four of them. Since they could not get him to Jesus because of the crowd, they made an opening in the roof above Jesus and after digging through it lowered the mat the paralyzed man was lying on. When Jesus saw their faith he said to the paralytic, "Son your sins are forgiven."

Now some teachers of the law were sitting there thinking to themselves, "Why does this fellow talk like that? He's blaspheming! Who can forgive sins but God alone?"

"Immediately Jesus knew in His spirit that this was what they were thinking in their hearts and He said to them, "Why are you thinking these things? Which is easier to say to the paralytic, your sins are forgiven, or to say get up, take your mat and walk? But that you may know that the Son of Man has authority on earth to forgive sins..."
He said to the paralytic,
"I tell you get up, take your mat and go home." He got up, took his mat and walked out in full view of them all. This amazed everyone and they praised God, saying, "We have never seen anything like that!"

Once you have made the decision to be a John 3:16 believer and start your journey with Jesus, there is something very important I want you to do right away. I want you to find the closest mirror you can and I want you to stop and look in the mirror. I want you to look yourself in the eye and I want you say, "Jesus has died for you, and He has forgiven you and I forgive you too!"

For some of you this might be harder than asking God for forgiveness. Guilt is a crippling emotion. It can destroy our self-esteem, paralyze our will to act and drive us into the depths of depression. It is every bit as crippling as the illness that paralyzed the man in the verses quoted above.

But the truth is just like the paralyzed man you have been healed, spiritually as well as emotionally. The question is, will you act like it.

When Jesus saw the man on the mat He was moved by his faith and the faith of his friends who carried him there. As a result He gave the man the greatest gift he could receive. His sins were forgiven. However, for the sake of those who were present Jesus also healed the man of his paralysis so by this miracle the people would know that Jesus was who He said He was and He had the authority to forgive sins!

What would have happened if when Jesus told the man to get up, take your mat and go home, the man would have just laid there? What if, even though he was healed he didn't believe Jesus, and as a result didn't act healed.

Not only would those present have thought Jesus was a fraud, but the man would have gained nothing. For even though he had the ability to walk he would still act paralyzed.

That is what refusing to forgive yourself could do to you. Leave you crippled and paralyzed and unable to fulfill the plans Jesus now has for you.

Now that you have joined Jesus on this journey He wants to take you to places your guilt wouldn't have allowed you to go before. He wants those around you to see a healed and whole person. He wants them to be amazed at the change in you just as the people who saw the man get up and walk were amazed.

Ephesians 2: 10 says "For we are God's workmanship created in Christ Jesus to do good works which God prepared in advance for us to do." God has been waiting for you to take this step and He has exciting and wonderful plans for what He wants you to do!

The only thing that can hold you back is you! Don't look back, at your old life and believe that's all there is. Believe God is the God of miracles and you are one of them and watch how far He will take you.

If you want a testimony for this, you can look at me. Never in my wildest dreams did I ever think I would be writing a book. In fact it never even entered my head to try. A few months ago I was sitting at a Christian convention listening to a Christian speaker talking about what a bad reputation Christians seem to be getting in this world and suddenly I turned to the person next to me and said I should write a book and call it <u>Don't Let Christians Keep You From Christ</u>! She looked at me and said you know I think you should, and here I am.

It would have been easy for me to say I'm not qualified to write a book, because in and of myself I'm not. It would have been correct to say I'm certainly not good enough to be writing a book about Christ, because I'm still a sinner. It would have been safer for me to say I didn't have time, or I had other priorities, because then I wouldn't have the risk of being rejected. Which, by the way, is still very much a possibility.

The truth of the matter is however, that I felt at the time and still feel today that this book is being given to me to write by God, and whatever success it has had will be done only if it is used to Glorify Him and help others to get to know Him.

God has things He wants you to do as well, but only if you are willing to get up, pick up your mat and walk.

I heard a testimony recently that both thrilled me and broke my heart. It was about a man who attended a speech given by Christian speaker. After the speech the man approached the speaker and told her God would never forgive Him. She told Him God could and would forgive him if he would just ask him. He told her she didn't understand, and it was not possible for him to be forgiven. She kept trying to get him to explain to her why it was impossible and finally he told her he was a member of the mafia, and it was his job to kill people, and he had been doing it for a very long time. She told him God would and did forgive even that. Finally he looked her in the eye and quietly repeated; I'm forgiven? She told him yes, you are forgiven! He leaped to his feet and shouted; I'm forgiven!!

He then took her hand and asked her to pray for him because he now was going to have to go to his bosses and tell them he was through. That God forgave him and he was never going to kill anyone again. He told her this even though both of them knew that no one ever quits the mafia.

I wish the story had a happy ending in this life, but the truth is the man did what he said he would do and as a result he was killed. However, I know that man was dead in his guilt long before he heard that woman speak, and he was never more alive than he was when he decided he would no longer live in bondage to that guilt. He was forgiven, he believed it, he embraced it, it gave him great joy and now he stands in the presence of his Savior Jesus Christ!

Who knows what effect the result of his decision had on those around him, but I am sure many of them were just as amazed as those who saw the paralyzed man walk. So, what do you think? What does God have in mind for you? Where will He take you? What will He have you say or do? It's exciting, I know, but it's kind of scary too. Just remember, whatever He has in mind, He's been planning it for a long time and knows with His help you are fully capable of doing it.

So get started, get up, pick up your mat and …….

Chapter 11: Fan the Flame

Acts 2:3

"They saw what seemed to be tongues of fire that separated and came to rest on each of them. All of them were filled with the Holy Sprit."

When I was growing up I used to work for my dad on weekends helping him clean a small office building. I had several jobs, which included dusting off the desks and sweeping the floor. The best job however was burning the trash. Every week we would collect all of the trash from the wastebaskets and separate out the burnable items and I would then put it all in a big metal drum behind the office building and burn it.

Depending on the weather conditions, it might take some time to get the fire burning, but once it was going I became fixated on keeping it burning until every little bit of trash was incinerated.

In order to keep it going it took a lot of attention. I had to stir it up and sometimes move the trash around to different spots, in order to make sure that it wouldn't go out. To keep it going I had to stay focused on the fire and it's condition.

I use to make a game out of it by seeing if once I had it started I could keep it burning until everything was gone without having to restart it. Now sometimes that was pretty hard. As I mentioned the weather would have a lot to do with it. If it was raining or really windy, it would be more difficult, and there were many days when I had to give up and leave some of the trash for my dad until the next night. After awhile, with practice, I became pretty good at fanning the flame and keeping the fire going. If you decide to enter into a relationship with my friend Jesus, then that should be your approach to maintaining and developing that relationship. You need to focus on keeping the fire going.

The verse I quoted at the beginning of the chapter talks about how the Apostles received the Holy Spirit after Jesus went to be with His Father. The Holy Spirit appeared to the Apostles as tongues of flame that came and rested on each of them.

When we accept Christ as our Savior we receive the Holy Spirit and we establish a link between the God that created the universe and us. When you stop and think about that, it's pretty awesome.

Many times when a person enters into a relationship with Jesus they become consumed with a desire to know more about Him. They read the Bible, they pray, they go to church whenever the doors are open, and they can't seem to get enough. However, over time, just like the weather conditions made it harder for me to maintain the fire in the drum, pressures of life and time constraints make it more difficult to keep our focus on our relationship with Jesus. Believe it or not, we can start to neglect our awesome opportunity of communicating with God. It's important to make sure that we keep the fire going, and that we keep feeding it fuel to make it even brighter.

One way that we can try to avoid this is by establishing a steady and consistent time when we communicate with God. Maybe you are a morning person so first thing in the morning would work for you. Or maybe you like the idea of spending lunch with Christ, or like me you might like to do it before you go to bed. The important thing is to set up a time a stay with it.

That doesn't mean that you need to spend hours a day in prayer. However the more time you can spend productively the more your relationship will grow. The key is to know what is productive for you. Some may feel renewed and energized by spending an hour in the morning praying and reading the Bible. For others, they may not have the time for that. I read the Bible and pray at night, but I spend a lot of time driving for my business so Jesus and I spend a lot of time in conversation during the day. Whatever time you decide to establish remember when you are trying to keep a fire going you need to steadily feed the fuel.

I would just caution that sometimes when you are trying to keep a fire going if you try to feed too much into at once you could force out all of the oxygen and can suffocate the fire. Make sure that you are taking the time you need to listen to what God wants to tell you and understand the things that you are reading. I believe that it's better to spend quality time reading a few pages rather than trying read too much at a time and not really understanding what we are reading. I have found that if I read just six pages in my Bible each day, I can easily read through the entire Bible in a year and I don't get overwhelmed. You may want to do more, or maybe less. Just make sure you have quality time with Jesus.

We need to pace ourselves in our communication with God in prayer as well. Make sure you take time to listen when you pray to Him as well. Also when you pray, be in tune to the fact that God can answer prayer and will answer prayer often times through other people. You may be surprised to find someone who has dealt with the same problem that you have, suddenly approach you. Don't be surprised it may just be God's way of answering you.

The flip side of doing too much that we don't absorb it, is assuming once we have a relationship with Jesus we don't need to do anything to maintain it. As I explained earlier, once you have a fire going you have to stay focused on keeping it going. If you fill up the drum and start the fire and walk away you run the risk of the fire going out, or worse having it fly out of the drum and burn out of control.

If we accept Christ as our Savior, but then walk away and forget about our relationship with Him we run the risk of having that fire go out too and we can miss the enormous blessings He has planned for us in this life.

I know in my own life when I lose touch with Jesus, and try to do too much on my own, that's when my life starts to fly out of control. When I focus on maintaining contact with Jesus and allow Him to call the play, then the relationship works and I continue to trust Him more and more.

One of the regrets I have in my life is I have had a lot of really good relationships that for whatever reason I have allowed to slip away. Whether it was friends I had in high school, the Navy, or college, at the time I thought I would maintain contact with these people forever.

However over time it is so easy to lose touch. At first you're talking everyday it seems, then it's every week, every month, and then finally you lose track altogether. Believe me, in today's world it is hard to maintain quality relationships with other people.

I do not want that to happen in my relationship to Jesus, however. It has become too important to me. I cannot imagine what it would be like to not have Jesus in my life. I see His hand in an active way every day. I don't always like what I see, sometimes His idea for the ways things should go don't always match up with mine, and yes, I'll admit it, there are some days I am angry with how things might turn out, but I would never want to lose touch with Him. There may be times during your relationship with Jesus when He will seem like He is very far away. Remember, He hasn't moved away, you have. He desires to have a vital and continuous relationship with us. He is never too distracted by the efforts of keeping the universe intact to stop and listen to us when we pray. He is never too busy with making sure that whatever it is that keeps atoms together doesn't disappear, to take time to comfort us during times of trouble when we need Him.

So as you take Jesus' hand and allow Him to lead you in this new adventure as a Christian, resolve yourself to hold on tight. Stay focused on allowing the time you need to let your relationship grow, and continue to fan the flame of fellowship and friendship with Him.

As we head into the last chapter of the book, we are coming full circle and we will again be talking about how Christians can often give Christ a bad name. However, as you decide if you want to enter into a relationship with Jesus, and take on the title of Christian we will be talking about how you might be able to reflect Jesus in a way that will draw your friends and family to Him, rather than drive them away.

We are going to talk about "Lighting the Light".

Chapter 12: Light the Light

Mark 12:30-31

"Love the Lord your God with all your heart and with all your soul and with all your mind and with all your strength. The second is this: Love your neighbor as yourself. There is no commandment greater than these."

How can we Christians truly reflect Jesus in a way that will attract our friends and family to Him as opposed to driving them away? I can give the answer to that question in one four letter word, LOVE! After all we are only saved by love, Jesus' love for us.

Jesus' love for us and our love for Him and through Him our love for others is the only true recipe for salvation. In 1 John 4:19 – 20 John tells us "We love because He first loved us". If anyone says, I love God, yet hates his brother he is a liar. So one of the byproducts of our new relationship with Jesus is we need to love. Love Jesus, love ourselves, love our family, and love our neighbors.

Earlier in the book I compared our reflection of Jesus to that of a fun house mirror. It was distorted by our sin. Well that's still true, however, the closest we come to accurately reflecting Jesus is when we love.

Webster's dictionary and the world in general have all sorts of definitions for love. So when I say that we need to love our neighbor, what kind of love am I talking about? Well Paul gives us a beautiful definition of love in 1 Corinthians 13: 4 – 7, "Love is patient, love is kind. It does not envy, it does not boast, it is not proud. It is not rude, it is not self-seeking, it is not easily angered, it keeps no record of wrongs. Love does not delight in evil, but rejoices with the truth. It always protects, always trusts, always hopes, and always perseveres."

Now that's love for you. If we can love like that, then maybe the reflection of Jesus won't be so distorted after all. The problem is; no matter how hard we try we won't always be able to love like that.

So another thing we need to do to be a good reflection of Jesus, is to be honest. We need to be honest with ourselves, and with others. We are not perfect, never have been, never will be. Christians get in trouble when they give the impression that because we are Christians we have it all together, and everybody else doesn't.

Now most of us don't TRY to give that impression, but somehow it manages to look that way. The reason why, is we don't want people to know that we're still sinners. We think that by being sinners we are failing Jesus, and that's what damages our witness. So the last thing we want anyone to know is what big failures we are. The problem is that's not true. The truth is, there are only two kinds of people in this world. Sinners, and sinners saved by the grace and love of Jesus.

So the best witness we can be is to let people know that we are just people. Fallible, insecure, emotional, people just like them. People who have found the love of Jesus in their lives, and it's His love that has made the difference not any effort on our part.

Now that's not to say that people shouldn't see a difference in our lives. When the Holy Spirit enters into a relationship with us He won't let us just stay the way we are. He wants us to be the best that we can possibly be, and I know that I want to be the best I can be because Jesus loved me! However, no matter how hard I try I will never be perfect and neither will anyone else.

So don't be afraid to be honest. Our friends and family need to know they can come into a relationship with Jesus right now! Exactly the way they are! Warts and all!

A third thing we need to do in order to be a good reflection of Jesus is to understand we are not Jesus! We cannot save anyone. There is only one savior, and it's not us. Now I know sometimes we want something so bad we feel that we just have to make it happen.

Sometimes that happens when we want someone to meet Jesus. Maybe that's what happened with you. Maybe someone wanted you to meet Jesus so bad that they practically beat you over the head with the Bible to try to make you understand. The problem is the harder they beat you with it the less you wanted to understand.

No matter how bad we want it, and no matter how hard we try, we can't make someone enter into a relationship with Jesus. That's hard to accept, but it's true, the sooner we realize it, the better.

What we can do is be a witness. Through the way we act, the way we love, and the way we live we can let people know who Jesus is and why they need to have a relationship with Him. We can always be ready to let people know why we feel the way we feel about Jesus, but we need to be sensitive to try to be aware of when people are ready to hear it.

Another thing we can do is pray. We can pray Jesus will make Himself known to others in ways we may not even be aware of. Once again I think we feel that if we don't make someone accept Jesus then they aren't going to. The truth is that Jesus really doesn't need us. He may want to use us to help some one meet Him or He may just want us to stay out of the way.

I have tried to make a point of praying for all my friends and family every day, and one of things I pray for is that they will either have a closer relationship with Jesus, or if they don't have one at all, that they will find

Him. I have been amazed by how often God has brought someone into a friend or family member's life from out of nowhere. Or they heard a song on the radio, or they read a book, and all of sudden they realized they were missing something.

It may have been the same thing that I told them they were missing five years ago, but they heard it in a different way, from a different person, and all of a sudden it made sense. So when you don't know what to do, pray! And when God suddenly makes something, magical happen, don't be surprised ....but I know you will be.

The name of this chapter is "Light the Light. Jesus said in John 8: 12, I am the light of the world. Whoever follows me will never walk in darkness, but will have the light of life.

If you walk with Jesus, then you walk in the light. However sometimes I think it's like we have a flashlight, but we hide it under our coat, or we forget to turn it on. The best way that we can reflect Jesus' is by letting His light shine through us. We need to reflect that light and brighten the lives of everyone we meet.

So how do we do that? By loving them, by being honest about ourselves, by understanding we are not their savior, by being a witness for Jesus' love, and by praying for them.

Now that's easy to write, but not so easy to live. However it is a recipe for success!

So how about you? Are you ready to take the next step? Are you willing to give Jesus a chance? I hope that by reading this book that you have a better understanding of my friend than you did before. I also hope that you will forgive all of us overzealous or underachieving Christians that have been giving Him a bad name.

Now is your chance to meet Him on your own terms. Pick up a Bible and start reading. If you don't have one, go to the library, or practically any Christian church and you can find one. Make up your own mind! After all, you are the only one that can.

Maybe, just maybe, you already have made up your mind. Maybe you would like to enter into a relationship with my friend Jesus right now! If that's the case I have included on the last two page of this book a simple process to ask Jesus to come into your life. It's called the Roman's Road because it uses verses from the book of Romans.

Either way I want you to start reading the Bible, I want you to start talking to Jesus, and I want you to take a chance. Take a chance that Jesus is who He says He is, and that He can do what He says He can do, and that He can and will change your life.

May God bless you and keep you all the days of your life!

Appendix

*Meeting Jesus,
Taking a walk down the road!*

In order to enter a relationship with Jesus, all you really have to do is ask Him to come in. However to make sure that you understand what He's asking you to do I have presented the following *"road to a relationship"*

1. **Understand that you are a sinner.**

   Romans 3: 23 "For all have sinned and fall short of the glory of God"

2. **Recognize that being a sinner separates us from God and eternal life with Him, but He gave us Jesus as a gift to bridge the gap between Him and us.**

   Romans 6:23 "For the wages of sin is death, but the gift of God is Eternal life in Christ Jesus our Lord."

3 **Understand that even though we are still sinners Jesus died for us, just the way we are!**

   Romans 5: 8 "But God demonstrates His own love for us in this:

   While we were still sinners, Christ died for us."

4. **Profess that in your life you believe that Jesus is YOUR Lord, and through the power God, His Father, He was raised from the dead.**

Romans 10: 9-10 "That if you confess with your mouth, Jesus is Lord, Believe in your heart that God raised Him from the dead, you will be saved. For it is with your heart that you believe and are justified and it is with your mouth that you confess and are saved.

5. That you understand the importance of obeying Jesus by being baptized as soon as possible.

Romans 6: 4 "We were buried with Him through baptism into death in order that just as Christ was raised from the dead through the glory of the Father we too may live a new life.

Printed in the United States
53355LVS00001B/52-153